THE BLEN

Blenders and j... world of exciting and ...
possibilities, and in this book is a varied
selection of tried and tested recipes, all of
them easy to prepare, thrilling to the taste
and naturally good for you.

THE BLENDER AND JUICER BOOK

Easy-to-prepare and Delicious Recipes

by

MAURICE HANSSEN

NATURE'S WAY

THORSONS PUBLISHERS LIMITED
Wellingborough, Northamptonshire

First published 1978

ISBN 0 7225 0388 1 (UK)
ISBN 0 89437 029 4 (USA)

Photoset by Specialised Offset Services Ltd, Liverpool
Printed and bound in Great Britain by
Weatherby Woolnough, Wellingborough,
Northamptonshire

CONTENTS

ACKNOWLEDGEMENTS

A special word of thanks to the two manufacturers of my own juicers and blenders. I have a Kenwood *Chef*, with juicer and blender attachments, and a Nature's Bounty *Three-in-One* continuous juicer, blender and shredder made by Rotel.

Both companies have very kindly allowed me to use or modify some of their recipes, and they have given me inspiration for a number more. As I have no commercial interest in either firm this brief word of thanks is given as freely as was their kind help.

Choosing and Using
Blenders and Juicers

Choosing and Using Blenders and Juicers

A blender is a relatively simple device consisting of an electric motor which drives a set of blades revolving in a glass or plastic goblet. But, despite this basic simplicity, the performance of different blenders varies widely. The reason for this is that the actual shape of the goblet and the precise design of the blades, as well as the power of the motor, have a profound effect on the efficiency of the various operations that the blender is called upon to deal with.

It goes without saying that the large firms who have spent vast amounts of time and money on research all market very good and reliable products. Indeed, when I visited the *Kenwood* factory I was most impressed, not just by their research but by the quality control that they have built in to every stage of the manufacturing process. All the big firms have a great deal going on behind the scenes.

You can buy for a fairly modest sum a machine that performs just the blending function and nothing else. A lot of such blenders have a small goblet on top taking about three-quarters of a pint (half a litre) of liquid, but these are not very easy to handle on the whole because frequently they are without pouring lips or handles, and are sometimes rather unstable. The more expensive models, however, usually have beautiful jugs on top of them and can take up to two pints (a little over a litre).

It is wise to look for a blender which has a small lid in the middle of the main lid as this will enable you to add extra ingredients without making a mess whilst the blender is in operation. If you are going to use hot liquids be sure to choose a model that has a handle; and look out for a scale of measurements on the side of the jug as this is of great help and saves making another utensil dirty. Variable motor speeds are useful if you are going to chop crumbs – which need a very low speed – as well as using the machine for liquidizing and blending.

A good blender will allow you to quickly prepare foods that are laborious and time-consuming in the usual way, and it will enable you to incorporate, for example, scraps and small pieces of food in an appetizing manner. Liquidized ingredients need very little cooking so they finish up more fresh tasting and, indeed, more nutritious than traditionally prepared foods. Other important uses include the preparation of high quality baby foods so that you really do know the quality of the ingredients you are giving to your child.

Also, there is a great cost saving to be made by using one power unit for many functions. That is to say, starting with a basic piece of equipment which has scope for the addition of various attachments. In this way you can build up the versatility of the machine to suit your requirements.

USING YOUR BLENDER

A blender can be used in many ways to help you, not only with the recipes in this book, but also to simplify your general cooking. For example, if you have a mixture of wet and dry ingredients it is often a good idea to blend the wet ingredients together before mixing in the dry in the usual way. Do not be afraid to experiment.

Be very careful when poking down inside the machine whilst it is running because if you go too far you will have a shredded spatula or wooden spoon – and this also tends to damage the machine! Be very sure never to go down more than three-quarters of the way and, better still, turn off the machine, give the contents a stir and then start it up again.

With very thick ingredients like mayonnaise the blades sometimes whirl an air space into which nothing seems to flow. You then have to keep stopping the machine, giving the contents a stir and starting up again. Often this problem can be solved by finding a speed at which a mixture begins to flow again when you can then trickle some salad oil in through the hole in the lid producing a perfect emulsion.

Many dry foods – in fact, the drier the better – can be chopped on the slowest speed. Useful examples include biscuit and bread-crumbs (at last you can keep a stock of wholemeal bread-crumbs!) herbs and nuts. The best way is to have the lid on with the central portion removed. Start the machine slowly and drop the ingredients through the hole onto the blades, quickly putting your hand back over the opening every time you let go of a piece so as to avoid having a stream of bread-crumbs hitting you straight between the eyes. The machine usually begins to labour when the goblet is between a quarter and a third full, when you will need to empty out and start again with the next batch.

Dried fruits, especially figs and dates, can glue a blender up alarmingly. The high sugar content combined with a fair degree of hardness produces a paste which jams up under the blades if you are not careful. A good idea is to warm such dried fruits slightly in the oven and they will become rather softer. Give the top of the mixture a helping turn with the spoon or spatula in the same direction that the blades are revolving. You may find it best to switch the blender off and on frequently, giving the mixture a good stir in between goes. This all sounds rather hard work when spelt out, but in fact the job is still quick and relatively painless. A good rule is that anything that you can cut with a knife can be handled by a blender, but if, as in the case of uncooked bones, a knife will not cut them – then please be kind to the blender.

Your blender is sure to come with a very carefully compiled and comprehensive set of instructions. An Austrian food scientist, an old friend of mine, who has invented many new recipes has often had calls from people who had not been successful in their attempts to make some of the recipes work. 'Madam, madam …', he would say, when reaching the end of his tether, '… if all else fails, please follow the instructions!' Every make of machine has its own individual preferences, so do please read the instructions carefully and then you will be sure to get the best out of your machine.

BUYING A JUICER
The two most important types of juice extractor are the centrifugal separators, which are continuous in operation, and those which are not, and which are called batch operation juicers.

On the whole the batch operation juicers tend to get more juice from a given quantity of material, but they do need cleaning out after every pound or two of material has been fed into them. Continuous operation juicers have various types of mechanism for ejecting pulp from one side of the machine whilst the juice is being poured from a lip on the other side of the machine.

I own one of each type, a *Kenwood* batch juice extractor and a *Nature's Bounty* continuous extractor. The great advantage of both of these machines is their versatility in other directions as well as performing very efficiently their juicing functions. For example, the *Nature's Bounty* machine has an attachment which shreds and slices salad materials, vegetables and fruits very rapidly and most attractively, so that cole-slaw or grated carrot becomes an easy task. This machine also has a very good blender attachment in the form of a glass goblet. I have had my machine for very many years and it has never let me down.

The *Kenwood* machine, on the other hand, is an attachment to the *Kenwood Chef* mixing machine. This is a wonderful tool which does everything from mixing dough to beating egg-white with great speed and efficiency. Other attachments that I use include a very powerful mincer, a coffee grinder, a blender of very high efficiency with a plastic and a glass jug of large capacity, and a flour mill with which I can freshly mill wheat for home bread making, as well as being able to grind any other cereals and pulses. Other attachments include a power-driven can opener, a slicer and shredder and a cream maker which homogenizes milk and butter to make a passable cream.

In our kitchen these two machines complement one another very well. For example when the apple harvest is good we often juice fifty to sixty pounds of apples in order to make apple juice for drinking fresh and for turning into apple wine. This would be a terrible job with a batch juicer, but is simplicity itself with a continuous machine. On the other hand the *Kenwood* is an incredible maid of all work, of beautiful design and construction at a very reasonable price.

Of course these two models are not the only makes worth buying. Machines used and recommended by people whose opinions I value include the *Bosch* and the *Braun*. The French firm of *Moulinex* produces a good batch-type juice separator, and *A.E.G.* and *Moulinex* both make a continuous model as well.

The thing to do is to establish what sort of machine would be most suitable for your purposes, and then choose a juicer which does nothing other than juice, or one which is part of a more complete set of equipment and has the price advantage that one motor is being used for many functions. Juicers are certainly worth shopping around for because quite staggeringly large discounts are often available, and it is rarely necessary to pay the manufacturer's recommended price.

Non-Alcoholic Drinks

Non-Alcoholic Drinks

Electric blenders and juicers open up a whole new world of exciting and delicious drinking sensations. With a good blender you can prepare wonderful natural drinks from the very best pure raw materials. The subtle fragrances and aromas of freshly blended or juiced ingredients cannot be captured by commercial producers. Such drinks nourish the cells of the body, rebuild your vitality and create freshness. Where preferred, yogurt and milk can add valuable protein and other nutrients to your drinks. Dried milk is easy to make up in a blender, but be sure to mix for only a few seconds or a froth will be produced which is very hard to lose. Use your imagination and experiment – develop your sense of taste and become a gourmet of delightful drinks. Makes notes in this book, adjusting the recipes to suit yours and your family's palates.

This section will be of special interest to teetotallers who must often get bored with the restricted range of drink ideas for their delectation compared to the almost limitless number of alcohol-based drinks.

Times are changing. 'One for the road' is bad news for drivers. Breath tests are causing wise drinkers to say 'No thank you' to alcohol many hours before the party is over. So, what does the host or hostess offer them? Usually orange squash or tonic water, or a cup of tea or coffee. How about providing delicious and wonderful non-alcoholic alternatives so that guests can see that you really care for their pleasures in a thoughtful way? It is easy to have a non-alcoholic bar, and with a blender or juicer you can provide a spectacular range of tastes. And, it is worth remembering that a superb drink can cost less than one that is mediocre.

Be particular over the ingredients, the mixing and the way you serve your drinks. Natural materials have natural variations in flavour and sweetness; so taste, test and approve in a creative way. In this way you will be participating in a creative art, one that is rightly appreciated by discriminating, thirsty guests.

Most commercial drinks are made either with refined white sugar or with saccharine. We who want to stay healthy try to cut down on sugar of all sorts as much as possible. Therefore, as a general rule in all the recipes, if you can train yourself to enjoy a smaller quantity of sweetening it is all to the good. Raw sugar contains a number of valuable minerals which are not present in – to use Professor Yudkin's phrase – 'Pure, white and deadly' refined sugar.

There are two good stock syrups containing unrefined ingredients that you can use but – as I say – please try not to have too much, even of natural sweeteners.

Honey Syrup

8 oz. (250g) raw sugar
8 oz. (250g) honey
1 pt. (500ml) cold water

Blend at medium speed until sugar is dissolved. Then allow to stand in a cool place. Store in the refrigerator and shake before use.

Raw Sugar Syrup

1 lb (500g) raw sugar
1 pt. (500ml) cold water

Blend at medium speed until sugar is dissolved. Then allow to stand in a cool place. Store in the refrigerator and shake before use.

I know that the metric equivalents are not precisely the same as the Imperial measures, but they are convenient and in the same proportions.

Love Apple Cocktail

The Love Apple was a name used by the English in the Middle Ages to describe the newly imported tomato. This is a rather refined and fine flavoured tomato appetizer.

2lb (1kg) ripe tomatoes
1 teaspooonful sea salt
6 teaspoonsful lemon juice
2 teaspoonsful raw sugar
1 teaspoonful Worcester sauce (optional)
pinch of basil (optional)

Purée at the highest speed for half a minute. Pass through a fine sieve to remove any seeds. Heat in a saucepan until simmering and then gently cook for three minutes. Cool thoroughly before serving.

Orange Reviver

2 oranges
$\frac{1}{2}$ lemon
1 free-range egg
4 ice cubes
1 teaspoonful raw sugar
$\frac{1}{2}$ pt. water

Choose unblemished oranges, preferably with a thick skin, and wash them thoroughly with a little unscented soap; then rinse to remove any chemicals from the outside. Cut the orange and lemon into small pieces and place in the blender with the other ingredients. Blend at high speed for twenty-five to thirty seconds. Strain, and serve cold.

Tomato Cocktail

8 oz. (225g) tomatoes
5 fl. oz. (150ml) unflavoured yogurt
¼ teaspoonful Worcester sauce

Blend the tomatoes until they are a fine *purée*. Add the yogurt and Worcester sauce (and, if liked, a few drops of lemon juice and two drops of Tabasco sauce). Blend again for ten seconds. Serve cold.

Caribbean Fantasy

1 banana
1 slice pineapple (optional)
½ pt. (275ml) cold milk
1 free-range egg
1 tablespoonful raw sugar
3 ice cubes

Blend at high speed for thirty seconds.

Orange Dream

5 fl. oz. (150ml) plain yogurt
5 fl. oz. (150ml) reconstituted, frozen or fresh orange juice

Best served really cold. Blend the ingredients together for thirty seconds, then serve into glasses. When used as an appetizer before lunch or dinner I find that a few drops of Angostura bitters produce a subtle and delightful aroma.

Kenwood Lemonade

This is one of the favourite recipes from the

Kenwood experimental kitchens. Instead of white sugar, however, we shall use raw sugar which retains some of the valuable minerals.

1 lemon
2 tablespoonsful raw sugar
6 small ice cubes
1 pt. (550ml) cold water
1 egg

Thick-skinned lemons are the best. You simply have to blend at high speed for ten seconds and strain into a jug. When you wish to serve the lemonade add some ice cubes and float some thin slices of lemon on top of the drink. Kenwood cleverly suggest the addition of a few sprigs of parsley which is, like the lemon, a great provider of Vitamin C and gives the lemonade a distinctive piquancy.

Lemon Squash

6 lemons
3 lb (1½kg) light raw sugar
4 pt. (2 litres) water

Take the outer peel from half of the lemons and blend with half a pint (300ml) of the water for thirty seconds at the highest speed.

Put the remaining water in a saucepan and add the blended lemon peel to it, and then bring to the boil. Juice all the lemons and add this together with the raw sugar to the mixture in the saucepan. Stir (not over the heat) until the sugar is dissolved then strain into hot clean sterilized bottles which should be sealed securely. Use as lemon squash, diluting in the normal way. If desired, the pulp of the lemons can be blended with the peel provided that the pips are removed before blending.

Minty Apple

1 large apple
juice of half a lemon
5 fl. oz. (150ml) water
2 ice cubes
2 mint leaves
1 oz. (30g) raw sugar

Remove the core from the apple and cut the rest into pieces. Put in the blender at top speed for thirty seconds with the other ingredients. Strain into glasses and serve with an additional sprig of mint.

Lemon Cordial

3 thin skinned lemons
2 pt. (1 litre) water
1 lb (450g) raw sugar

Quarter the lemons, add half a pint (275ml) water, and blend at high speed for ten seconds.

Pour into a saucepan and add the remaining water and the sugar. Stir until dissolved, then gently bring to the boil. When cool strain into bottles. The lemon cordial should be kept in a refrigerator and diluted as required.

Orange Cordial

3 thin-skinned oranges
1½ pt. (¾ litre) water
12 oz. (350g) raw sugar

Cut the oranges into quarters and mix together with half a pint (300ml) water. Blend at high speed for ten seconds.

Pour into a saucepan and add the rest of the water together with the sugar. Stir until dissolved then bring to the boil. When cool strain into bottles which should be stored in the refrigerator and diluted as needed. Some people prefer the orange cordial to have a little added lemon juice.

Lavish Lemonade

10 lemons
2 oranges
10 oz. (250g) raw sugar

Thinly skin two of the lemons and one of the oranges and blend with one cupful (10 fl. oz. or 250ml) water at high speed for twenty seconds.

Add the water-and-peel blend to the sugar. Heat gently, stirring all the time, in a heavy saucepan. Simmer for five minutes. Allow to cool thoroughly. Use your juicer or otherwise extract the juice from the insides of the oranges and lemons, add to the syrup, then store in a bottle in the refrigerator. This is a particularly fine tasting lemon squash which can either be diluted with water or used to flavour other things.

Peach Affection

1 lb (450g) stoned, peeled and chopped peaches
5 oz. (150g) raw sugar
3 tablespoonsful honey
10 fl. oz. (250ml) water
1 pt. ($\frac{1}{2}$ litre) orange juice

Heat the honey, sugar and water together until dissolved. Allow to cool. Blend the other ingredients together, add the syrup. Serve very cold. The drink can be sprinkled with cinnamon and cucumber.

Summer Delight

1 lb (450g) carrots
3 apples
3 sticks celery
$\frac{1}{4}$ bunch watercress
pepper and sea salt to taste

Chop the ingredients into pieces and blend altogether until smooth.

This is also very effective made in a juicer, in which case put the watercress through first and the carrots last.

Green Glory

5 tablespoonsful chopped parsley
1 Avocado pear
1 cucumber
juice of a lemon
1 tablespoonful corn oil
2 cupsful crushed ice

Peel the cucumber and the avocado then blend altogether and serve garnished with thin slices of lemon.

Tomato Enchancer

1½ lb (750g) tomatoes
1 medium-sized green pepper
1 medium-sized onion
½ teaspoonful dried basil
1½ tablespoonsful Worcester sauce
3 tablespoonsful lemon juice
1 dessertspoonful corn oil

Seed the pepper, and skin the tomatoes, then liquidize until very smooth. Frozen tomato pulp is very good for this recipe so that you may enjoy it in the spring. (See below).

Some years we have a wonderful crop of tomatoes. Quite a lot of them grow so fast that we have no time to eat them in their best fresh state. Some we scald and peel and then deep freeze, others, when time is not on our side, we quickly do the blender way. It seems to me now though that the blender way is about as good as the laborious, scalding method. Just put the whole tomatoes in the blender at high speed for a minute. Before freezing it is a good idea to simmer them gently until the volume of the tomato pureé is reduced to about a half of the amount you started with. So long as you cook fairly carefully the flavour seems to stay the same, but you have not got to freeze large quantities of water.

Lemon and Molasses Drink

2 lemons
1 pt. (550ml) water
3 tablespoonsful molasses
6 ice cubes

Juice one whole lemon and take the juice of another. Add the water, molasses and ice cubes, and blend for thirty seconds. Serve cool.

Molasses Banana Shake

10 fl. oz. (275ml) milk
2 bananas
2 tablespoonsful molasses
pinch sea salt

Blend for thirty seconds and serve at once.

Hot Spicy Milk Shake

10 oz. (275ml) milk
1 tablespoonful molasses
sprinkle of cinnamon, allspice and nutmeg

Heat all the ingredients together and blend for ten seconds before serving.

Molasses Milk Shake

1 pt. (550ml) milk
4 tablespoonsful molasses
nutmeg

Make sure the milk is very cold, and blend with the molasses for twenty seconds at top speed. Pour into glasses, sprinkle with nutmeg and serve.

Hawaii Five O

1 pineapple (peeled)
juice of a lemon
4 tablespoonsful raw sugar

Juice the peeled pineapple. Add the lemon juice and blend with the sugar. Serve with ice.

Morning Glory

1 orange
½ a lemon
white of an egg
1 cupful of ice cubes

Juice the orange and half lemon. Add the egg white and cupful of ice cubes. Blend at top speed for thirty seconds, and serve.

Grape Highball

red or white grapes
honey
lemon or lime juice
egg white

Juice some red or white grapes, and to every glassful add one teaspoonful honey, the juice of one lime or lemon and one egg white. Blend these ingredients at top speed for twenty seconds. Serve with added ice and soda water.

Driver's Gimlet

juice of half a lime (or half a lemon)
a little Angostura bitters
1 teaspoonful syrup
4 ice cubes
1 egg white

Blend for ten seconds at top speed, strain and serve in chilled glasses.

Plum Fizz

Stone and juice 2 lb sweet plums. (If you have no juicer this can be done by simmering with four tablespoonsful of water in a covered pan and then allowing to strain through muslin. The residue can be used for jam making.)

1 pt. (550ml) plum juice
8 oz. (225g) raw sugar
2 teaspoonsful cider vinegar
1 pt. (550ml) soda water

Dissolve the sugar in the warm plum juice, stir in the cider vinegar. Chill, and add soda water at time of serving.

Banana Home

1 egg white
1 banana
5 fl. oz. (150ml) grapefruit juice
3 strips each of orange and lemon peel
ice

Blend the egg white at a high speed for fifteen seconds, then add the other ingredients and blend again. Serve with added ice when really nice and foamy.

Watercress Wonder

1 pt. (550ml) pineapple (or orange or grapefruit) juice
1 bunch watercress
juice of half a lemon
2 tablespoonsful syrup
3 ice cubes

Blend all the ingredients together, except the ice, until the watercress is blended in. Add the ice cubes one at a time through the lid until they are also blended, then serve at once.

This recipe is a wonderful way of enjoying the mineral and vitamin C rich watercress which imparts a delicious tangy flavour to the pineapple or other citrus juices.

Tomato Orange Freshener

1 pt. (550ml) tomato juice
½ pt. (275ml) orange juice
2 tablespoonsful lemon juice
2 slices onion
¼ teaspoonful sea salt
3 ice cubes

Chill all the ingredients thoroughly. Blend at top speed for thirty seconds. Serve really cold – a wonderful appetizer!

Lemon Froth

3 fl. oz. (75ml) lemon juice
2 egg whites
4 oz. (100g) honey
12 fl. oz. (350ml) water
2 ice cubes

Blend together for about thirty seconds at top speed or until very frothy. Pour into cool glasses making sure that everyone receives a fair share of the foam!

Fruit Frappés

A *frappé* is an almost frozen drink that is very acceptable on a hot summer's day.

Frappé recipes are best done by volume. A cup of ice cubes should be blended slowly until mushy. Then add, whilst mixing, a cup of fresh, chilled, fruit juice. As soon as the ingredients are mixed serve into ice-cold glasses. Sometimes a touch of syrup to sweeten or a little lemon juice to sharpen will improve the flavour of the *frappé*, but this is for your individual preference.

Ginger Man

This is a great combination for lovers of ginger. You will need:

4 halves of dried apricots
8 fl. oz. (225ml) grapefruit juice
2 teaspoonsful honey
2 dessertspoonsful ice cubes
1 teaspoonful chopped crystallized ginger (or $\frac{1}{4}$ teaspoonful powdered ginger)

Soften the apricots in the water for half-an-hour or so, then blend with the grapefruit juice and honey. When thoroughly mixed add the ice and ginger. Blend briefly and serve with more ginger sprinkled onto the drink.

Mint Julep

This is one of those soft drinks that goes really well with savoury dishes.

4 sprigs of mint
1 pt. (550ml) white grape juice
pinch sea salt
6 oz. (175g) cubed pineapple
juice of a lemon
5 dessertspoonsful grapefruit juice

Use only the leaves of the mint. Put them in the blender with the other ingredients and liquidize fast until the mint is thoroughly combined with the other ingredients. Add some ice and serve in wine glasses.

Orange Slimmer's Drink

This is one of the nicest low-calorie summer drinks.

1 pt. (550ml) orange juice
6 oz. (175g) soaked dried apricots
2 tablespoonsful lemon juice
½ pt. (275ml) crushed ice

Put all ingredients together in a blender, set at high speed and blend for twenty to thirty seconds, or until there is a good froth on top. Serve at once. A touch of Angostura is an enjoyable addition. Two drops in the glass before pouring are enough.

Apple Juice Drinks

Apple juice is easily made by putting the whole apples, pips and core as well, into your juicer. Apples are so easy to obtain all the year round that I do believe it is worth while using them if you can.

These drinks also taste good made with

bottled apple juice but be sure to choose a make that you know to be reliable because the cheaper apple juices tend to have a cooked flavour which quite destroys the usual refreshing taste.

Apricot and Apple Drink

1 cupful dried apricots
2 cupsful apple juice
2 cupsful crushed ice

Soak the apricots for half-an-hour or so in the grape juice until they are soft. You can do this in the blender. Add the ice, and blend until smooth.

If you like, you can add either some cinnamon or a little nutmeg before serving.

Ginger Apple

2 cupsful apple juice
1 cupful cherry juice (it is best to remove the stones before juicing the cherries)
1 oz. (30g) crystallized ginger (if you have only powdered ginger allow ½ teaspoonful to soak in the juice for 1-2 hours before making the drink)

Mix everything together in the blender until it is smooth. If you like, a little extra ginger can be grated on top.

Pineapple and Carrot Drink

1 pt. (550ml) pineapple juice
½ lb (275g) chopped raw carrot
1 tablespoonful lemon juice
a pinch of basil or tarragon

Blend all the ingredients at high speed until completely smooth.

Pineapple Fizz

½ lb (225g) raw sugar
½ lb (225g) honey
1 pt. (550ml) water
1 pineapple
10 fl. oz. (275ml) soda water
ice

Dissolve the sugar and the honey in the water. Put in a heavy saucepan and boil until the mixture is slightly heavy and syrupy. Allow to partially cool.

Peel the pineapple and cut it into small squares. Place in blender and liquidize at high speed for 30 seconds together with enough syrup to cover the pineapple (you will probably have to divide the quantity into several portions in order not to overload the blender). Let the mixture stand in a cool place for three or four hours, then strain. Chill thoroughly before serving.

Do not leave overnight in a warm place or else the mixture will ferment.

Early Riser

1 lb (450g) carrots
1 lemon
2 eggs
4 tablespoonsful milk
1 teaspoonful raw sugar

Juice the carrots and lemon, then place all ingredients in the blender and liquidize until smooth. This takes about thirty seconds. Serve very cold. If made the night before this makes a delightful instant breakfast.

SODA WATER DRINKS

I wonder if you have considered the ingredients in commercial fizzy drinks? They often contain a quite extraordinary number of additives in the form of thickeners, stabilizers, colours, artificial sweeteners and flavourings. For this reason people concerned with good health say: 'Sparkling drinks are bad for you.'

So long as they are pure I believe that there are few drinks more refreshing on a hot summer's day than a sparkling, natural cool and delicious long drink.

There are on the market several brands of soda syphon which you can re-charge yourself and these represent a great cost saving. I have a *Sparklets* – which is available in most parts of the world – and find it very satisfactory after many years of use.

But for sheer convenience and variety there is to my mind nothing to touch the *Sodastream* machine which is available in more than 170 countries. This has a large and economical container of carbon dioxide and small re-usable split-sized bottles which you fill with water, insert in the machine and aerate – then just add a measure of whatever flavouring you fancy. A lot of the squashes and cordials in this book are ideal. All the family can have a few bottles of their favourite variety kept in a cool place so that when they come in hot and tired a delicious drink is immediately ready.

The makers of the *Sodastream* do have their own range of concentrates to produce various drinks such as Indian Tonic Water and ginger beer but for commercial reasons, so as to match the taste of the shop-bought equivalents, they obviously contain artificial flavours and, where necessary, colours.

If you have no machine, then use ordinary bottled soda water, but do read the list of ingredients to make sure that it does not contain any undesirable additives. I am a firm believer in controlling the quality of what we eat so far as possible by using raw materials of known quality.

Hot and Cold Soups

Hot and Cold Soups

Summer Strawberry Soup

Have you ever thought of strawberry soup as a starter? It needs to be served ice cold and often leaves guests guessing as to what went into it.

1 pt. (550ml) chicken stock (or strong vegetable stock)
½ lb (250g) strawberries
½ teaspoonful powdered ginger
sea salt, black pepper, chopped fresh mint
5 fl. oz. (150ml) natural yogurt

Liquidize everything except the yogurt, then simmer very gently for just four or five minutes. Allow to cool, blend in the yogurt, chill very thoroughly. Sprinkle the mint over as a garnish before serving.

Summer Pea Soup

This soup can be enjoyed hot or chilled and so can be quickly adapted to suit a sudden change in the weather.

1 lb (450g) young fresh green peas
$\frac{1}{4}$ lb (100g) peas in their shells
7 oz. (200g) spring onions with good green stems
6 oz. (175g) vegetable margarine
2 cloves of garlic, chopped
5 fl. oz. (150ml) thick cream
chopped fresh herbs as available such as parsley and chives

Take all the margarine and melt it in the thick pot in which you gently *sauté* the onions and garlic, making sure that they do not go brown. This takes three or four minutes.

Add all the peas and also the peas in their pods (choose the best looking ones for this purpose) together with $1\frac{1}{2}$ pints (a little less than a litre) of water. Simmer for five to ten minutes until the peas are just beginning to soften, then blend for thirty to forty seconds.

Add all the cream just before serving, then decorate with herbs.

Vichyssoise Soup with Radishes

6 oz. (175g) radishes
2 large leeks
1 tablespoonful vegetable oil
6 oz. (175g) cooked potato
$\frac{3}{4}$ pt. (425ml) stock
5 fl. oz. (150ml) milk
2 tablespoonsful thick cream
sea salt and black pepper

Slice the leek and the radishes. Fry both in the oil very gently until they are soft but not coloured. Liquidize all the ingredients together for about a minute, adjust the seasoning and serve hot or cold.

It is worth remembering that you nearly always need more seasoning when a soup is to be served cold than when it is hot.

Gazpacho Soup

Our Spanish gardener, José, a small wiry man of indefatigable energy, loves to revive himself with this gazpacho recipe.

Make sure the tomatoes are really ripe – the purist will not only peel them but remove the seeds, although I find it just as good using frozen or tinned tomatoes, which although peeled still contain all the seeds.

2 lb (1kg) tomatoes
bunch spring onions
3 green peppers
2 cloves garlic
$\frac{1}{2}$ cucumber
1 thick slice bread
1$\frac{1}{2}$ pt. (1 litre) chicken or clear vegetable stock
5 tablespoonsful vegetable oil
sea salt
black freshly milled pepper
4 tablespoonsful cider vinegar
1 teaspoonful raw sugar
2 tablespoonsful chopped parsley
1 teaspoonful basil (if available)

Take the flesh from the peppers and chop it coarsely. Dice the peeled cucumber. Chop the spring onions, retaining as much of the green as possible. Crush the garlics. Remove the crust and soak the soft part of the bread in a little cold water, wait a minute, squeeze and add to the other ingredients. Mix everything together in a bowl, except the stock, then, making sure that it is not more than half full, put into the blender. Blend for only five seconds. This is to make sure that you have a very coarse *purée* with pieces of vegetable still visible. Empty the blender into the serving bowl and then go on blending until all has been done – making sure never to blend too long.

Add the chicken or vegetable stock, adjust seasoning and check for the acidity which should be just noticeable If you like, a little lemon juice can be added). Gazpacho needs to be chilled for several hours before serving and can conveniently be prepared well in advance of the meal.

It is customary to accompany gazpacho with little dishes containing attractively and finely chopped vegetables such as more green peppers, cucumbers and tomatoes together with some croutons of fried bread.

Orange and Carrot Soup

This seems an unusual combination but the two flavours blend together well and are fine for a cold starter on a hot summer's day.

1 lb (500g) young carrots
1 onion
1 tablespoonful vegetable oil
1 teaspoonful raw sugar
juice of 4 large oranges
$\frac{1}{4}$ pt. (150ml) double cream
chopped chives or spring onion tops
sea salt, pepper
$1\frac{1}{2}$ pt. (1 litre) chicken or clear vegetable stock

Finely slice, or coarsely grate, the well-washed carrots and, with the chopped onion, stew in a covered pot for ten to fifteen minutes with the oil. Be sure not to allow the vegetables to brown at all.

Add the stock, seasoning and sugar and simmer on a tiny heat until the vegetables are soft – this may take from 30 minutes to an hour.

Blend the soup as soon as it is a little bit cooler. Add the orange juice and allow to cool completely. Gently stir in the cream. Make sure that the soup is really chilled before serving, when a final garnish of chopped chives or spring onion tops produces a very pretty soup. You can also sprinkle a few grains of paprika on top if you wish.

Yogurt and Cucumber Soup

This delicious cold soup has a touch of the Balkans or the Middle East about it.

$\frac{1}{2}$ pt. (275ml) yogurt
1 medium-sized cucumber
vegetable or chicken stock
5 tablespoonsful thick cream

Peel and slice the cucumber and blend with the yogurt and an equal volume of stock.

Season to taste with some sea salt, freshly ground black pepper and a pinch of brown sugar. Allow to become thoroughly chilled. Then stir in the thick cream very gently, to leave a spiral pattern stretching across the soup from the centre. Chill again, then decorate with the chopped green parts of spring onions or chives before serving. Alternatively sprinkle with chopped fresh mint with a dusting of paprika.

Scotch Broth

When used as main course these quantities are about right for two people.

1 pt. (500ml) water
1 lb (550g) lean minced beef
1 large carrot
1 medium-sized potato
1 large onion
1 medium-sized turnip
1 cabbage or lettuce leaf
1 oz. (30g) barley
$\frac{1}{2}$ teaspoonful sea salt
pepper, parsley and other herbs to taste.

Simmer the beef with the seasonings for fifteen minutes in a pint of water.

Coarsely cut the vegetables, then put them into the blender, cabbage first. Cover with water and blend at high speed for just five to ten seconds.

At the end of the cooking time for the beef add the vegetables to the meat in the saucepan, together with the barley and any water that is left over. Simmer gently for thirty to forty-five minutes.

Taste and make any seasoning adjustments that are necessary, and serve sprinkled with fresh green parsley.

Nettle Soup

1½ lb (675g) young nettle tops
1 pt. (550ml) milk
sea salt, pepper
2 tablespoonsful wholemeal flour

After washing the nettles cook them very quickly for ten minutes with the lid off in a pan containing a pint (550ml) of boiling water and a little sea salt.

Add a pint of warm milk to the strained nettles and put them in the blender together with sea salt and pepper to taste and the wholemeal flour.

Return the blended mixture to the saucepan and simmer gently until the soup has thickened when it is best served at once.

Green Pea Soup

This is a family recipe from Somerset which is known to have been made since 1770.

4 pt. (2 litres) peas
5 pt. (2½ litres) water
sprig of fresh mint
1 stick celery
2 large Cos (Romaine) lettuces
¼ lb (125g) butter or vegetable margarine
2 large cucumbers
2 or 3 large onions
pepper and sea salt to taste

Shell the peas, reserving the best looking shucks. These should be boiled separately with a little of the water and strained into the soup to give it a better colour. Put the peas, mint, celery and shredded lettuce, pepper and salt into the water and cook until tender. This takes about twenty minutes. Strain most of the liquid off the soup into a separate container and blend the remains until they are smooth. Skin and seed the cucumbers and cut them into pieces about half-an-inch thick. Roughly slice the onions, shred another large Cos lettuce, cook in the butter or margarine until soft, then put everything together in the soup pan and add, if desired, a few extra small peas. Simmer very gently for half-an-hour. Thicken with a roux made from wholemeal flour and margarine, with a little of the stock added to it, and simmer until thick. If you like, you can garnish the soup with slices of cauliflower and cucumber.

Foamy Cream of Sorrel Soup

Guérard often uses a liquidizer in his slimmers haute cuisine recipes and, although many of the best blender dishes do use lots of cream, there is no doubt that a fine dispersion of fresh, light ingredients enhances the flavour in a way which means that heavy, high-calorie ingredients can be dispensed with without loss of quality.

$4\frac{1}{2}$ oz. (125g) fresh sorrel
2 cloves of garlic
$1\frac{3}{4}$ pt. (1 litre) chicken stock
2 teaspoonsful olive oil
$1\frac{1}{2}$ teaspoonsful sea salt
pepper
2 eggs

Heat up the oil in a saucepan, crush the peeled cloves of garlic with the blade of a knife and brown them lightly in the oil.

Add the roughly chopped sorrel, sea salt and pepper and stir. Put in a little of the chicken stock and cook gently for fifteen minutes.

Pour this mixture into the blender and liquidize for about two minutes in order to obtain a completely smooth liquid. Put the soup back into the saucepan and heat it until it is just beginning to boil.

Just before serving you must whisk the two eggs in a bowl until they are very light, and then quickly add the hot but not boiling soup, whisking briskly all the time. Because the eggs are aerated by the whisking they set on contact with the hot soup and make the resultant dish light and delicious.

Superb Savouries

Superb Savouries

Taramasalata

This Greek recipe was given to me by an expert wine maker and gastronome, Pano Tsergas, who was one of the best practical chefs I ever met. So often the recipes for Tarama (which is really a smoked cod's roe mayonnaise) produce rather disappointing results, but empty dishes at many parties have led me to the firm belief that this recipe is the one that pleases most people! Smoked cod's roe usually comes in little plastic pots containing about 5 oz. (150g). If you buy cod's roe by the piece and remove the skin then you can push it into a container that it fills completely and use that as your guide. So the recipe is based on a pot containing about 5 oz:

1 portion smoked cod's roe
3 portions corn oil
1 large squeezed lemon
1 thick slice of bread, soaked in a little milk and gently squeezed
1 small onion

Blend the bread and milk, add the onion so that it too is finely minced together with a portion of the oil. Blend again. Add the roe and lemon-juice and stir so that the mixture is easily distributed, then, while blending at a medium speed, add the rest of the oil in a gentle trickle. If your blender is working well, it will transform the mixture into a beautiful creamy mayonnaise with a delicate pink colour. If your blender cannot take this quantity easily, then halve the ingredients and make two lots. Serve the Taramasalata with hot wholemeal toast. By the way, Tarama keeps for at least a week in a cold refrigerator, but deep freezing is not recommended.

Quick Chicken Liver Pâté

3 fl. oz. (75ml) corn oil
1 lb (500g) chicken livers
2 oz. (50g) butter
4 oz. (100g) mushrooms (thinly sliced)
4 oz. (100g) crisp fried bacon (finely chopped)
2 oz. (50g) fresh wholemeal breadcrumbs
brandy or port
seasoning

Heat the corn oil in a stout saucepan and, when ready, cook the chicken livers, turning frequently until well done. This takes about six minutes.

Purée the contents of the pan in the blender, return to the pan and then warm over a very low flame. Add the butter, bacon and raw mushrooms. Season to taste. Add whatever herbs take your fancy (fresh if possible) together with the breadcrumbs.

Keep the mixture on the verge of simmering for five minutes, stirring all the time.

Add a generous splash of brandy or port, then turn out into the serving bowl and stir occasionally as it cools before putting it to cool in the refrigerator where it will set.

Smoked Mackerel Pâté

12 oz. (350g) smoked mackerel
4 oz. (100g) cottage cheese
4 oz (100g) vegetable margarine
juice of half a lemon
5 fl. oz. (125ml) single cream

This beautifully mild and fishy *pâté* makes a wonderful start to a formal dinner, or is very good as a party snack or savoury.

Choose fat, healthy looking smoked mackerels. Skin and bone them and divide the fish into fairly small pieces.

Add all the other ingredients, with – if you wish – a grating of fresh black pepper, then mix well. Put the mixture in the blender and liquidize until all is evenly combined into a smooth cream. Chill (when the *pâté* will set) and serve with wholemeal toast, decorate with slices of freshly cut lemon.

Meat Loaf

1 lb (500g) finely minced lean beef
1 lb (500g) finely minced lean pork
2 wineglassesful red wine (optional)
3 eggs
1 large onion
2 cloves garlic
handful of parsley
1 teaspoonful thyme
½ teaspoonful oregano
1 teaspoonful sea salt
black pepper

Put everything except the salt, pepper and
meat into the blender, and blend until
smooth. Mix with the meat and season to
taste. Put the mixture into an oiled bread tin
and bake for an hour at 325°F (165°C) mark 2.
This can be eaten hot or cold and is very good
for picnics. It seems to me that shop-bought
meat loaves contain far too much fat and
gristle, so this is the way to control this
undesirable situation to the benefit of your
health and to the pleasure of your palate.

Savoury Meat Spread

Your blender will make quick work of
leftover meat, and with it you can produce
some delightful sandwich fillings.

1 cupful finely chopped cooked meat
2 tablespoonsful cider vinegar
1 chopped onion
1 chopped garlic clove
2 gherkins
1 tablespoonful corn oil
A good splash of red wine, or sherry or grape juice

Put all the dry ingredients into the blender and then slowly add the vinegar, then the oil and mix until it thickens. It is possible that you will need an extra tablespoonful of oil – but see how it goes. Leftover vegetables can be added to this recipe and indeed with plenty of vegetables you can leave out the meat! Put in the wine or juice last.

Some Dhals

Dhal is an Indian word covering a wide variety of lentils and seeds. The poor often just eat unleavened bread moistened with a good dhal and with this simple mixture obtain not only much needed calories but also vital protein. Some dhals are dry or are cooked whole, but with a blender you can make many delicious dhals that go well with, as you would expect, curries, but also are very good with any savoury dish or with a wholemeal spaghetti. These recipes will give you some ideas – you may then make up some of your own, depending on the ingredients that are available.

Basic Dhal

8 oz. (250g) lentils
½ teaspoonful turmeric
1 tablespoonful vegetable oil
1 teaspoonful chilli powder (may be omitted if not desired)
½ teaspoonful ginger powder
1 good-sized onion (peeled)

Carefully rinse the lentils in cold water. Cover the lentils with plenty of water (2 pt. or 1¼ litres) add the turmeric and simmer gently, removing any scum from the surface from time to time, until the lentils begin to soften.

Fry the onion in the oil until it becomes slippery and translucent, then add the chilli powder and ginger and stir for a moment. Take the frying pan away from the heat. Blend the lentil mixture until it is smooth, add the mixture from the frying pan (being careful that the hot oil does not splash you) and your dhal is ready to enjoy.

Sweet and Sour Dhal

8 oz. (250g) lentils
2 pt. (1½ litres) water
½ teaspoonful turmeric
½ teaspoonful ginger
juice of 2 lemons (or 4 tablespoonsful cider vinegar)
2 teaspoonsful raw sugar
2 tablespoonsful vegetable oil
½ tablespoonful cummin seed
1 teaspoonful ginger

Wash the lentils carefully in cold water then simmer with the turmeric and salt until the lentils are tender. Blend for a while until the mixture is very smooth. Put in the raw sugar, lemon juice or cider vinegar and ginger powder and simmer for a further four or five minutes whilst you heat the oil in the frying pan and cook the cummin seed for a minute or two. Add the oil and seed carefully and your dhal is ready to serve.

Dhal Cakes

6 oz. (200g) lentils
1 teaspoonful chilli powder
1 teaspoonful cummin powder
1 teaspoonful curry powder
sea salt
vegetable oil
1 lb (500g) wholemeal flour

Wash the lentils and then soak them overnight when they will swell up. Drain off most of the water then liquidize until smooth, adding the spices at the same time. Make the wholemeal flour into a fairly flexible dough with some water and knead it very thoroughly. Leave the pastry to season for an hour or so and then knead it once more.

Break off pieces of dough, slightly larger than a walnut, and with your thumb press a hole into the middle. Fill this with the dhal mixture, capture the dhal inside the dough by smoothing it over and then gently flatten. Deep fry the ready-made cakes in hot vegetable oil until they are crisp golden and beautiful.

Apart from yellow, green and red lentils (all of which have a distinctive and delicious flavour) for dhals you can use the beans the Indians called Urid and Mung. A good Indian shop will also have a number of other pulses (sometimes as many as fifty) for you to try. Mung and Urid beans when sprouted make the most delicious bean sprouts.

Pear and Spinach Purée

3½ oz. (100g) pears
14 oz. (400g) fresh spinach (or beet tops will do)
sea salt and pepper

Peel, quarter and core the pears and cook for fifteen minutes in some boiling water. Remove the thick stalks from the spinach and wash the leaves. Cook them for just three minutes in sea salted boiling water. Rinse the spinach with cold water and then drain very thoroughly. Liquidize the spinach and pears together with a little seasoning which should be adjusted to taste. This needs to be served at once.

This recipe is by Michel Guérard. He is famous for his *Cuisine Minceur*, which is to say slendering food. Most of his recipes are made from pure, natural ingredients and his book makes interesting reading.

Cheesey Omelette

(per person)
2 eggs
1 tablespoonful milk
1 oz. (30g) cheese (small pieces)
sea salt and pepper

Put all together in the blender and liquidize for a minute. Then make your omelette by heating oil in a well seasoned or non-stick frying pan. As soon as it begins to set, lift the edge up by means of a wooden spoon or other non-scratching implement, allowing the uncooked egg to run underneath. As soon as the top is almost set, close the omelette and fold it away from the handle straight on to the plate. Omelettes need to be served at once. If they are kept too long or (and this is the most common fault) they are overcooked, they assume an unappetizing appearance and the consistency of well-matured leather.

Various Other Omelettes

With the blender you can incorporate many other flavours to make omelettes more exciting. Apart from cheese flavours those that are best incorporated during blending are herbs, onions (a good mixture is one chopped onion and one teaspoonful of parsley), and fish omelettes in which a little cooked white fish or salmon is added to the mixture in the blender at the rate of about 2 oz. (30g) per person.

Those ingredients which are best added whilst cooking is proceeding include mushroom, ham, asparagus, Spanish (mixture of peppers, sweetcorn (maize), peas, ham, prawns or indeed anything vaguely exotic in sight). For Spanish omelettes the ingredients which require more than very light cooking need to be prepared beforehand.

Sweet omelettes still need a bit of salt but can do without the pepper. You can fill them with delicious home-made raw sugar jams, nuts, cooked drained fruit, raisins and sultanas and so on.

Dips, Dressings and Sauces

Dips, Dressings and Sauces

Parties are fun with dips, and quite often potato crisps are used as a scoop to convey the dip to the mouth. Some commercial crisps are very pure and indeed, in order to save money peeling them, they are frequently made from very thinly sliced, washed, unpeeled potatoes. Health for economic reasons! These are then cooked in vegetable oil until very crisp and then allowed to dry on absorbent paper. You can make these very easily for yourself. Sprinkled with a little sea salt you have what our forefathers called 'game chips', their invariable accompaniment to partridge and grouse.

You can toast wholemeal bread, remove the crusts and cut into thin fingers and, provided the loaf is well made, these are delicious and nourishing dip sticks.

For the sake of attractiveness the dips can

be put in prettily coloured pottery containers or into drinking glasses and decorated with fresh salad vegetables, which, in the case for example of strips of turnip, celery, cauliflower florets, cucumber and carrot can be used instead of the bread or the chips for dipping.

Garlic Cheese Dip

8 oz. (200g) cream cheese
1 small chopped onion
2 crushed garlic cloves
½ teaspoonful Worcester sauce
2 oz. (50g) grated Parmesan cheese
6 fl. oz. (150ml) creamy milk
a little sea salt

Put the milk into the blender, and add the cheese and onion a little at a time. If the dip is too thick add a little more milk. The dip should be the consistency of double cream.

Roquefort Cheese Dip

4 oz. (100g) cream cheese
2 oz. (50g) Roquefort cheese
2 tablespoonsful milk
a little finely chopped onion or garlic
1 tablespoonful port wine, or red wine

Blend together briefly, adding more milk if necessary. Cool thoroughly before serving.

Curry Dip

Make thick mayonnaise the blender way (see pages 69-70). To each cupful of mayonnaise stir in two heaped teaspoonsful of curry powder. Allow to stand for several hours before serving to give time for the flavours to blend.

Balkan Dips

In the Balkans and in Eastern Europe sour cream is much used in cooking and gives a sharp tangy flavour which is most refreshing. If you cannot obtain specially soured cream but do have your own yogurt maker, you can culture an ordinary tub of double cream with a little yogurt. Stir well and allow to remain at 70°F (20°C) for twelve hours, then allow to settle in a refrigerator before using.

The sour cream can be lightly blended with a variety of different mixtures for example:

Chive Dip

4 oz. (100g) cream cheese
4 oz. (100g) sour cream
2 tablespoonsful chopped fresh chives
a little sea salt

Garlic Dip

4 oz. (100g) cream cheese
4 oz. (100g) sour cream
3 cloves crushed garlic
sea salt and freshly ground black pepper

Cucumber Dip

Blend together 6 oz. (150g) of peeled chopped cucumber which has been sprinkled with salt and then drained for an hour. A teaspoonful of chopped parsley, a teaspoonful of clear honey and a touch of onion can be added if liked.

Olive Dip

6 oz. (150g) sour cream
3 oz. (75g) chopped green olives
a little grated onion
sea salt and pepper

Blend all together.

Carrot Dip

4 oz. (100g) sour cream
4 oz. (100g) cream cheese
2 oz. (50g) grated carrot

Blend for a few moments and, if liked, add a little onion. This can also be used as an excellent stuffing for green peppers which then need to be chilled and thinly sliced for serving.

Paprika Dip

This can be made with either sour cream or mayonnaise. In either case add a little salt and blend in a heaped teaspoonful of paprika to every five fluid ounces (125ml) of sour cream or mayonnaise. This looks pretty on an assortment of dips as does the next which can be made just the same way.

Tomato Dip

Use a tablespoonful tomato *pureé* the same

way as the Paprika Dip recipe above although a little lemon juice or extra salt is sometimes needed to bring out the flavour.

Blender Dressings for Salads

For some reason or other not all oils seem to thicken mayonnaise as well as I would wish, and there seems to be inconsistencies between different bottles of similarly labelled oils. Nevertheless there are two types of oil, corn (or maize) and peanut (or groundnut) oil that are very reliable. Once the emulsion has started to be formed then you can stop using that oil and go on for example to safflower or sunflower seed oils if you wish. Olive oil is very good but often has, for my taste, too strong a flavour unless you have a really good first pressing virgin oil from a reliable supplier.

Mayonnaise (1)

2 egg yolks
2 fl. oz. (0.3 litres) corn oil
1 tablespoonful cider or wine vinegar or lemon juice
½ teaspoonful raw sugar
½ teaspoonful mustard powder (if desired)
sea salt
pepper

Mayonnaises are best made at room temperature so do not take any of the ingredients straight from the refrigerator. Put in all the ingredients except for the oil. Blend at maximum speed and, as soon as the blending has started, gently allow the oil to trickle into the mixture through the hole in the top of the blender. Alternatively you can put all the ingredients in together and blend, but some people prefer the consistency achieved by the first method.

Mayonnaise (2)

2 whole eggs
1 tablespoonful cider vinegar
sea salt and pepper
$\frac{1}{2}$ teaspoonful mustard powder
10 fl. oz. (250ml) corn or olive oil

Make as in the first of the two methods above.

Mayonnaise (3)

2 egg yolks or 1 egg
2 tablespoonsful lemon juice or cider vinegar
$\frac{1}{4}$ teaspoonful raw sugar
$\frac{1}{2}$ teaspoonful sea salt
1 teaspoonful mustard powder
10 fl. oz. (250ml) corn oil

Blend all the ingredients except the oil at top speed for forty-five seconds then add the oil in a steady stream through the hole in the lid while continuing to run the blender.

French Dressings

The classic French dressing often contains as many as six parts of oil, preferably olive, to one part of wine or cider vinegar. I find that much too heavy. It masks the flavour of the delicate salad vegetables. A little garlic often does wonders, if you like it, in a salad dressing and you can vary the quantity to your taste. Try adding a little lemon juice. Some sea salt and a few twists of freshly ground black pepper. You can vary the mixture between equal quantities of vinegar and oil (corn oil is very light and well flavoured) down to the French level. In all cases the smooth French dressing is made by blending for ten seconds or so at the high speed.

My Favourite Dressing

This dressing was first described in *Hanssen's Complete Cider Vinegar* and many people were kind enough to say how much they enjoyed it. For the flavours to marry you need to prepare it at least an hour before the meal, give it a quick blend then leave to stand, stirring before adding to the salad – this should be done either at the table or just before. You will need:

3 tablespoonsful corn oil
1 tablespoonful cider vinegar
squeeze of lemon juice
1 large crushed clove of garlic
a turn of freshly ground black pepper
pinch of raw sugar
pinch of mustard powder
some mixed herbs (see below)

For the mixed herbs I keep two assortments in screw-top jars. They are a little different from each other and I use what I fancy to suit the dish. They are:
Mix A: Parsley, tarragon and balm, chervil, chives, dill, thyme, basil.

Mix B: Parsley, dill, celery leaf flakes, tarragon.

The herbs are listed in roughly descending orders of quantity first largest, last least.

On the other hand if you want to just use the basic French dressing mixture of say, three parts oil to one part vinegar, then you can be flexible in the seasonings you choose. Basil, a neglected herb, goes very well with anything containing mushrooms.

Banana Dressing

2 tablespoonsful cider vinegar
1 tablespoonful corn oil
pinch of sea salt and pepper
$\frac{1}{2}$ teaspoonful mixed herbs
1 banana

Blend at top speed for thirty seconds for a lovely and unusual dressing. If you wish, you can add chopped nuts or small pieces of lean ham.

Yogurt Salad Dressing

5 oz. (125g) carton plain yogurt, or roughly this amount
$\frac{1}{2}$ carton cider vinegar (using yogurt carton)
$\frac{1}{2}$ carton corn oil (using the same carton)

You can use this as it is or with added herbs. If preferred a clove of garlic may be added before the ingredients are put into the blender. Blend at top speed for fifteen to twenty seconds.

Italian Pesto Sauce

This is delicious with wholemeal spaghetti, either as a main course or as a starter.

3 fl. oz. (100ml) vegetable oil
1 dessertspoonful vegetable margarine
2 dessertspoonsful hazlenuts or pine kernels
1 teaspoonful chopped basil
3 teaspoonsful chopped parsley
1 teaspoonful chopped oregano
2 to 3 cloves of garlic
4 oz. (100g) grated Parmesan cheese
sea salt, freshly ground pepper

Blend for about a minute then simmer very gently indeed in a saucepan until the sauce is heated through, taste and add a little salt and pepper to make the seasoning just right. This, like most Italian sauces, can be prepared in advance and heated shortly before serving.

Italian Nutty Sauce

For wholemeal pasta.

3 fl. oz. (100ml) milk
1 teaspoonful marjoram or oregano
sea salt
black pepper
4 oz. (100g) shelled hazlenuts
1 medium slice wholemeal bread
3 fl. oz. (100ml) cream

Soak the bread in milk. Put all the ingredients, except the cream, into the blender, blend for thirty to forty five seconds (a little less if you wish to retain small pieces of nut). Transfer to a saucepan, warm up, but do not boil, stir in the cream shortly before serving.

Hot Chilli Sauce

4 hot red chillis (including seeds)
2 large onions
1½ lb (675g) peeled tomatoes
3 tablespoonsful raw sugar
3 tablespoonsful sea salt
12 fl. oz. (350ml) cider vinegar

Simmer all the ingredients together for an hour, allow to cool a little then blend on a high speed for thirty seconds. Bottle whilst still hot, and cover at once.

This is a hot spicy sauce very popular at parties.

Chilli Sauce (II)

This is a very hot and spicy sauce wonderful with cheese and cold meats. But to be healthy be sure to remove any extra fat from the meat before you eat it.

1 pt. (550ml) cider vinegar
4 oz (100g) peeled and cored apples
4 oz. (100g) skinned tomatoes
3 oz. (75g) raw sugar
½ chopped onion
4 garlic cloves
2 tablespoonsful chilli powder
2 tablespoonsful sea salt
1 teaspoonful mace powder

1 teaspoonful tarragon powder
1 teaspoonful nutmeg powder
1 tablespoonful wholewheat flour

Simmer all together for an hour, stirring fairly often. Blend at high speed for thirty seconds. Bottle and cover whilst still hot.

Puddings and Desserts

Puddings and Desserts

Raspberry and Strawberry Fool

1 pt. (550g) strawberries
1 pt. (550g) raspberries
6 oz. (175g) raw sugar
1 tablespoonful lemon juice
1½ pt. (1 litre) cream
strawberries and raspberries for decoration

Juice the fruit, or blend it with the lemon juice and then strain. Add the sugar and lemon juice, then blend together with the fruit pulp or juice and the cream. Decorate with alternate raspberries and strawberries. Serve in individual tall glasses.

Gooseberry Fool

This can be made the same way, but it is best just to blend the gooseberries and not to juice them as they have a beautiful flavour which seems to be lost when juiced. Taste the blended gooseberries and, if they seem a little chewy, simmer them for a few minutes until they have softened. Then wait until they have cooled before trying them in the recipe.

Lord John Russell's Pudding

This old recipe came from Esher in 1863.

1½ pt. (1 litre) milk
1 oz. (30g) powdered gelatine
1½ oz. (50g) raw sugar
1½ pt. (275ml) cream
1 wineglassful brandy (or 2 wineglassesful white wine)
any assorted dried fruit that you have

Blend the egg yolks and the milk with the grated peel of a lemon, the gelatine and the sugar. Put in a heavy saucepan and whisk until the gelatine is dissolved and the mixture has thickened.

Add the cream and the brandy then, being sure not to allow the mixture to come to the boil, keep it hot for a while and stir as it thickens. Stir in some dried fruit and, if you have any, some chopped candied fruit (some health stores now supply fruit candied with raw sugar) put the mixture into a mould and cover with aluminium foil or greaseproof paper. Refrigerate for six hours.

Some Syllabub Recipes

Syllabubs are one of the oldest British desserts, and really consist of creamy milk set with wine, sherry or lemon juice.

They can be made without a blender, but if

blended I have found the results to be far more reliable and consistent than when mixed by hand. The actor Robert Morley said they are one of his favourite desserts, and he is a great connoisseur of puddings!

Lemon Syllabub

1 pt. ($\frac{1}{2}$ litre) single cream
3 lemons
$\frac{1}{3}$ pt. ($\frac{1}{4}$ litre) sherry (or $\frac{1}{2}$ sherry and $\frac{1}{2}$ brandy)
1 tablespoonful sugar

Use the rind of two of the lemons and take the juice from all three. Blend together until it has formed a froth, then pour into the serving dishes and allow to stand in a cool place for from between twelve and twenty-four hours.

Whipped Syllabub

$\frac{1}{2}$ pt. ($\frac{1}{4}$ litre) sweet white wine
1 dessertspoonful lemon juice
2 dessertspoonsful raw sugar
1 pt. ($\frac{1}{2}$ litre) single cream

Blend all together, put into serving glasses, and allow to stand for twelve to twenty-four hours in a refrigerator before serving.

Everlasting Syllabub

(From *The Compleat Housewife*, by Eliza Smith, 1727)

$\frac{1}{2}$ pt. (275ml) cream
$\frac{1}{4}$ pt. (150ml) Rhine wine
2 tablespoonsful sherry

1 lemon
4 oz. (100g) raw sugar

Whip and sweeten the cream. Beat in the
wine and sherry, the juice and grated rind of
the lemon. Whip for thirty minutes. Fill
wineglasses with your syllabub which is best
when three or four days old.

This works very well in a blender and can
be done just as Mrs Smith recommended!

Farmhouse Syllabub

1 pt. ($\frac{1}{2}$ litre) beer (brown ale is good)
1 pt. ($\frac{1}{2}$ litre) cider
4 pt. (2 litres) milk
a little nutmeg
4 tablespoonsful raw sugar

Blend together then let stand in a cool place
until set. Traditionally the syllabub was then
sprinkled with currants that had been
simmered in a little white wine or strong
beer!

London Syllabub

1 bottle port (or 1 bottle white wine)
4 oz. (100g) raw sugar
grated nutmeg to taste
1$\frac{1}{2}$ pt. (1 litre) cream
2 lemons

Grate the rind of the lemons and add it to the
wine. To each pint of wine add 1$\frac{1}{2}$ pt. (1 litre)
of cream at blood temperature, then pour on
the juice from the lemons from a height and
let it stand for two hours. Then blend it until

there is a froth, which you reserve. Pour the remainder of the liquid into serving glasses, top with the froth and allow to stand in a cool place for four or five hours before serving.

Hurried Cake Filling

When you have made a delicious wholewheat cake, a really moist succulent yet healthy filling is often just what the family craves.

6 oz. (175g) honey
6 fl. oz. (175g) sunflower or corn oil
1 free range egg

Blend together at medium speed for about twenty seconds. This can be used alone or can be varied, for example, by the addition of dried fruits or nuts.

Zabaglione

1½ tablespoonsful sugar
3 large egg yolks
marsala wine

This famous dessert is normally rather a laborious affair made over a double saucepan. It consists of egg yolks, sugar and marsala wine. To be honest, gastronomically speaking, there is no real substitute for this recipe which is made by whisking the egg yolks with the sugar over hot water until the mixture becomes lighter in colour, then adding the marsala wine (at the rate of 5 fl. oz. (125ml) for every 3 egg yolks) very gently whilst continuously whipping, so that you finish up with a wonderfully light confection, quite dry and beautiful.

Nevertheless, with our blender we can do a pretty good job.

Cold Zabaglione

2 fresh eggs
4 dessertspoonsful raw sugar
2 fl. oz. (50ml) marsala wine (or sherry)
2 fl. oz. (50ml) white wine
a banana or a wineglassful orange juice or a little lemon juice
2 ice cubes

Blend together for forty-five seconds and serve at once.

Warm Zabaglione

3 egg yolks
3 teaspoonsful raw sugar
3 fl. oz. (75ml) marsala wine
2 fl. oz. (50ml) white wine

Put the egg yolks into the blender together with the sugar. Blend for just a moment then, while the machine is still running, very slowly add the hot marsala and white wine which you can mix together. Continue blending until the mixture is quite light and foamy.

Pear Ice Cream

2 lb. (1kg) ripe pears
8 oz. (250g) light raw sugar
4 egg yolks
½ pt. (250ml) cream
2 tablespoonsful lemon juice

Slice the peeled pears, sprinkle them with the raw sugar and lemon juice and leave for at least one hour.

Beat or briefly blend the egg yolks, warm the cream until it is almost, but not quite, boiling, then quickly pour on to the egg yolks, stirring all the time in a bowl. Place the bowl over a pan of gently boiling water and continue to cook, stirring all the time, until the mixture thickens. Allow to cool a little then put the egg custard together with the pear mixture into the blender goblet and liquidize thoroughly. Freeze in a suitable container then, when the mixture begins to set, blend again and return quickly to the freezer.

Melon Water Ice

4 oz. (100g) light raw sugar
½ pt. (250ml) water
a ripe melon weighing about 1½ lb (750g)
3 tablespoonsful lemon juice

Make a syrup by boiling the sugar and water over an even heat for five to seven minutes. Allow to cool. Then quarter the melon, removing the pips and skin. Liquidize the melon flesh. Add the syrup and lemon juice to the blender and blend briefly again. Freeze and, as soon as the mixture begins to become solid, blend again and then quickly put back into the freezer.

Melon water ice is better taken out of the freezer at least quarter-of-an-hour before serving.

Joyful Juices

Joyful Juices

By the use of a juicer you can extract the quintessentially valuable components of fresh fruit and vegetables, allowing yourself far more beneficial qualities than would be possible if you were to eat your way through a comparable quantity of the actual unjuiced material.

Juices have, for very many years, been used therapeutically. They are certainly enormously effective in rebuilding shattered constitutions brought about by the polluted environments in which we are all forced to live. Many diseases and run-down conditions are cured through the medium of the wonderful natural agents that are present. For a full discussion of the therapeutic uses of juices I must recommend you to read *The Complete Raw Juice Therapy* by Susan E. Charmine (Thorsons).

Here though, we are concerned with the

pure unalloyed enjoyment of juices. I have explained elsewhere how you may choose the best juicer for your needs, but in fact you can obtain a lot of pleasure from even the simplest device, even though the advantages of a really good machine are unquestionable.

Unless you are sure of the origin of your raw materials do wash them in cold water and, in the case of root vegetables like carrots, give them a good scrubbing – *but do not peel* for it is near the surface that many of the more valuable nutrients are to be found.

Apple Juice

The perfect accompaniment to a fine summer's day is a glass of chilled, freshly expressed apple juice. Apples produce copious quantities of juice which blends well with almost any other fruit or vegetable. There is a lot of pectin in the apple which means that it also contributes valuable fibre to the diet and is easy to digest. With your juicer you do not have to peel or core the apples. Simply remove the stalk, cut into suitably sized pieces and juice away.

One of the main problems with apple juice is that the enzymes present tend to cause the juice to brown quite quickly. So there are two precautions that you can take. The first is not to cut up apples too long in advance of the actual juicing; the second is that you can add a little lemon juice or vitamin C to the container in which you are collecting your apple juice and this will prevent oxidation.

The *wrong way* to solve the problem is to heat the juice because although this is effective, the taste is quite spoilt. You will find this if you taste a cheap commercially bottled apple juice. Very expensive and superior makers such as *Schloer* do not cook their juices but sterilize them through special filters.

Other high class juices are prepared by means of pasteurization which prevents too much heat being applied for too long. But there is no question that fresh juice contains far more active and healthy nutrients than does any bottled juice and is, into the bargain, both cheaper and tastier.

Beetroot Juice

Wash fresh young beetroots well and brush them carefully to remove any earth otherwise the flavour from the juice reminds one distinctly of the soil.

I find it best to cut the beetroot into slightly smaller pieces than necessary for many softer vegetables, but this will depend on your machine. Beet juice has a gorgeous red colour and tastes well either alone or in combination with two thirds of orange juice, or with carrot and celery juice.

Berry and Soft Fruit Juices

Berries and soft fruits are sometimes a little

difficult to juice because of their high sugar content which can jam the machine. This is a particularly severe problem even with continuous juicers which often become clogged up if more than about a pound and a half (750g) is juiced at a time. So do remember to take off the lid and clean out the juicer rather more often than you would with other materials.

Good juice can be prepared from all edible soft fruits and berries such as blackberry, bilberry, raspberry, strawberry, redcurrant, blackcurrant and gooseberry.

Because of the good strong flavour these juices can often be effectively diluted in a mineral water, or indeed ordinary water. Sometimes you will need to add a little raw sugar or honey to taste and occasionally with very sweet fruits, a touch of lemon juice brings out the flavour.

Cabbage Juice

Both white and red cabbages make an excellent juice when used in combination with others, especially apple and orange. Cabbage juice is particularly good for people with weak digestions and is known to be able to alleviate gastric ulcers. The darker the green, the more the vitamin A content of the cabbage – but cabbages contain many other valuable nutrients as well, so enjoy them as a drink.

Carrot Juice

Carrots alone make a fine flavoured juice. It is best served rather cold and often improved by the addition of a little Worcester sauce. Carrot forms the basis of many excellent cocktails, try it with tomato juice, with a third of celery juice plus a little lemon. Taste a half-and-half mixture of apple and carrot juice. The most nutritious carrots are those that are dark orange or yellow in colour and, to my taste, these have a slightly richer flavour.

Celery Juice

Celery juice possesses a rather stronger flavour than you would expect from the somewhat watery consistency of celery stalk. It is always improved by adding a little lemon or other citric juice to it. Some people think that the green celery produces a rather superior juice, but I find them both fairly similar. Celery is a tasty addition to almost any vegetable juice mixture.

Grapefruit Juice

This is delicious by itself and also wonderful in combination with either vegetable or fruit juices. A particularly good mixture is half-and-half celery with grapefruit. Because the grapefruit is so soft you need to feed it in rather slowly, as with any softish fruits.

The skin of the grapefruit contains a substance called naringin, thought by some to be slightly toxic, so maybe it is better to skin your grapefruit first.

Orange Juice

Oranges can be juiced skin and all but be sure to wash them very carefully first because of the preservatives so often used to stop them from going bad.

Lemon Juice

Lemons make a different sort of juice depending on whether you just use the pulp or the whole of the lemon, try both and see which you prefer. Lemons often contain a chemical coating on top of the skin to stop them going bad, so be sure to scrub them very carefully if you are going to use the whole fruit.

Cucumber Juice

Like marrow juice, cucumber juice is extremely boring but can be used as a natural way of extending the volume of other vegetable juices. Cucumber juice also goes quite well with some fruit juices, the flavour of the one enhancing the other.

Tomato Juice

You do not need to remove the skins of tomatoes before juicing them, such a chore at other times. If you choose a really ripe and well-flavoured tomato the juice is probably one of the most beautiful of all. A little bit of sharpness in the form of lemon juice, or the addition of Worcester sauce, produces a typical tomato cocktail. If too thick, thin with water or apple juice. I know of no juice which does not combine well with tomato and you can also use tomato juice as a stock in which to cook sea food or other savoury dishes.

Parsley Juice

Parsley is very rich in vitamin C and the juice also contains many valuable minerals. It goes well with most other vegetable juices and can be taken by itself – or with water – because the flavour is quite strong.

Parsley Lemonade

To make two pints of parsley lemonade you will need about three bunches of dark green, fresh parsley. The best way to prepare it is to fill the feeding channel of the juicer up to the top with parsley before switching on the machine, then switch it on to full speed and very quickly plunge the parsely down on to the rotating blades as quickly as you can. As soon as you have juiced the parsley run the two pints of water through the juicer, this will remove all the juice, add raw sugar and lemon juice and you have a refreshing and health-giving summer drink.

Index